BY THE SAME AUTHOR

Four Dozen Short Poems

The Diary of a Curious Man by Patrick Black,

edited with a Foreword by Leo de Freyne

LANIAKEAN FRAGMENTS

Leo de Freyne

LULU

First Edition 2018

ISBN 978 – 0 – 244 – 70697 – 5

Our galaxy is in Laniakea.

Laniakea is a Super-Cluster of approximately a hundred thousand galaxies.

The name Laniakea, from the Hawaiian, means ‘immense heaven’.

THE PROSE

The greatest freedom is freedom from memory.

“We can do another course of chemotherapy.”

“No thanks.”

When someone dies, they become a fictitious character. Fictitious characters can be supportive, just as imaginary friends can be for children.

Your trillion thoughts about what happened is the present.

Of what will happen is the present.

Things either connect or not.

The price of death is life.

A knight on a black square can move to a white square only; a knight on a white square can move to a black square only.

Self-interest and empathy hold an uneasy truce.

These are the reasons people go on living:

1. Living is involuntary. Your lungs go in and out without permission.
2. Family.
3. Religion.
4. Work.
5. Diversion.
6. Various combinations of the previous five.

An ancient writer probably declared that the past is stored in the moon and the future is stored in the sun.

Nature knows no cliché; without cliché, there is no art.

Reputations are constantly under re-appraisal. So a writer can be considered established when no longer read.

"Dry your tears. It could be worse. You could be me," the dying person said.

If just some people died, how terrible our lives would be. It is death that makes survival bearable.

Pride is the face of the will to live.

Most of our troubles derive from the high value we place on our self-esteem.

You can be deprived of everything except your death.

“My bones are very near my skin now.”

Death is not the problem; suffering is the problem.

“Listening to beautiful music makes you think there’s something more…Something more than saying goodbye.”

You live in the present because there is nowhere else to live.

Order and chaos are different visions or interpretations of the same thing.

Drawing a tree, the artist has to balance the branches with the roots, even though the roots are largely hidden.

Every leaf is different. And they are not perfectly symmetrical.

Bad art is a hobby. Mediocre art is a career.

"It's a big step, dying."

Photography is the art of seeing an image; painting is the art of making an image.

Everything an individual experiences is stored in memory. Only a tiny fraction (triggered by feeling) is ever consciously retrieved. Very often, it is not obvious why a particular experience, sensation or sight is recalled; the connection with the present moment is not clear. Memory-links in the chain from the present moment to the past moment are not recalled.

"How are you?"

"Not too worse."

The soul does not exist, that is why the painter tries to paint it.

A loved one's dying and death is the profoundest experience there is. One's own dying and death will confirm this.

It is a form of good luck: having the opportunity to experience such bad luck.

One person's life is another person's theatre.

"Goodbye God," the dying person said.

"I think I'm turning to stone."

"My hand needs a lot of sleep."

"My arm needs a lot of sleep."

People talk of 'happy memories', but they mean 'memories of past happiness', for how can any memory be said to be happy?

Immature artists compete with each other; mature artists encourage each other. The former concentrate on being artists; the latter concentrate on art.

A sobering aspect of grief is getting over it little by little. One feels that it shouldn't be. One should have died of weeping.

One is dying of breath.

Noctilucent cloud: cloud so high it is illuminated by the sun during the summer night.

Being loved is easier than loving because loving is an active, uncertain practice.

All political Constitutions are works-in-progress.

No peace without hypocrisy.

Some people haven't a drop of despair in their veins.

When one human being is hurt by another, the 'hurtee' frequently responds by becoming a 'hurter'. Often the new 'hurtee' is not the original inflictor to the new 'hurter'. Thus a chain of hurting is constantly having links added.

A person who rationally chooses to die regards suicide as another action, the last action to be performed. Thus, the action will be automatic; analogous to the action of turning off a cooker or flushing a toilet.

A sign of growing old is not forgetfulness, but no longer caring about forgetfulness.

Grains of sand drift across the surface of the sand; a few grains catch the sunlight: they're the famous ones.

Inexperience is lack of lack of understanding.

There is the realisation that what you do is not of the same level of interest to other people as it is to yourself.

You do not fully exist in anyone's mind except your own.

Weeping is exhausting, but it leaves less energy to be depressed.

We have but one advantage over future generations: we are alive.

Love is the delusion that another person can free you from yourself.

If nobody makes you laugh, you'll just have to make yourself laugh.

It is of more use to be an Anti-Theist than an Atheist.

“Hell is other people,” wrote Jean-Paul Sartre. So when a young child asks where a dead person has gone, it is simplest to tell the child the truth: the dead person has gone to Heaven.

Is there life after death? Yes, but not for you.

It is okay to talk to yourself, but you are mad if you talk to yourself in public. The public does not like to feel it is being parodied.

Originality can be appreciated centuries after; originality remains original.

The purpose of art isn’t to show that the artist can make art. The purpose of art is to communicate feeling.

Feelings cannot be defined; they can be felt or not felt.

The writer’s first reader is the writer. The writer who is sensitive to the medium, namely language, will make every effort to isolate and weed out possible misunderstandings. Teaching children to read and to write is not enough. Teaching children to read what they write cultivates accuracy of communication.

The downside of being dead is that you can't enjoy it.

We speak of someone 'being' dead. We say someone 'is' dead. We use the verb 'to be' for the absence of 'to be'.

Some things are too simple to be comprehended.

To be in love with someone is to believe they are under-appreciated.

To be in love is to be in a state of adoration, yet fear of being banished by the adored.

The overly-sentimental and the grotesque are the two extremes of art.

A true anarchist is of the centre.

Sperm and ovaries. Such a lot of fuss.

There is no release from the State, not even by death.

Of all the illusions of permanence, art is the greatest.

There are three basic choices in politics: Democracy, Dictatorship or Civil War.

All drawing is drawing from memory.

Quality of brushstroke is like the difference in movement between a hesitant cripple and an Olympic ice-skater.

In politics, it's numbers that matter. Politics is the attempt to organize, manage and improve the State. Numbers can be counted, feelings cannot.

Most liberals can be defined as people who are not actively anti-liberal.

Women are not the opposite sex. Women are the parallel sex.

Religious education is the promulgation of ignorance.

When skill becomes habit it produces dull art.

"That's it! That's a life! We've got a wrap!"

Despite what Picasso said, all children are not artists; they are artistic, which is not the same thing.

Your closest friend reminds you that you are alone.

A rare escape from the self is joining with others in the conviction that justice can be achieved if we are willing to make the effort.

Malevich wanted to free art from 'the burden of the object'. Would it not be a good thing to free art from the burden of words?

You have to be deluded by someone to love them. And, after that, you have to know much about someone to continue to love them.

It is particularly difficult to sustain a friendship between a man and a woman who are not lovers because, when they fall out, no reconciliation via physical intimacy can take place. Such a love is often ephemeral compared with family or sexual love, because the participants have no securities in the bank.

Aloneness is the viewpoint of dreams. It is always 'I dreamt', never 'we dreamt'.

Indifference is two-edged. Healthy and cruel.

Is it not wonderful that everything turns out to be over? The freedom of it.

We keep things for others to get rid of when we die.

It is more accurate to say “I love her” or “I love him” than “I love you”.

One of one’s hands comforts the other hand of one’s hands.

Reflective intelligence in an animal’s body: this is the human condition.

Death is not the opposite of life; it is the end of life. The opposite of life is non-life.

The widest gulf is not between life and non-life, but between the past and the present.

The notion of ‘being creative’ is recent. It is doubtful anyone said to Raphael or Watteau “You’re very creative”. The same applies to ‘self-expression’.

Why do little girls, far more than boys, skip as they walk?

What happens is that you are here one day and another day and many days, and then one day you are not here and you do not know you are not here because you are not here.

Death stirs the pot.

Nationalism is the sludge encrusted in a stagnant drain.

May your indifference be positive.

No wisdom can detach us from feeling. Buddhism is a pursuit. All pursuits are pastimes.

The body is the problem; it gets in the way of death.

Due to human frailty, religion will never disappear; but confronted with ridicule and reason, religion will be recognised for what it is. To prevent this, religionists endeavour to institute 'blasphemy' laws and to suppress the teaching of real science. Their aim is to protect their position as promoters of the nonsense which is a major cause of human misery. Any comforts of religion, alas, go hand in hand with anti-human, anti-animal wishful thinking.

When you are depressed, you are depressed all the time.

What we love most is innocence. It restores the now; dispels the past and future.

Art is the way we slow down the dream.

It is said that 'Less is more', but 'Less is enough' is enough.

Too much conviction is as unhelpful as none.

Hora incerta, mors certa. Why wait?

To love someone, you need to be desperate.

Visual art touched its limit in 1915 with Malevich's black square, but that doesn't mean everything has been done.

"I don't give a damn" means "I don't want to give a damn".

Which came first, the chicken or the road?

Philosophy is to Theology as Astronomy is to Astrology.

It is not global growth we need, but global stability.

Anyone intelligent knows that the more the population increases, the more human suffering increases.

God is an idea. Ideas cannot be erased, but they can be categorised.

When they put their hand on you, you are surprised and therefore don't immediately react. After a few moments, they take their hand away. Because you have not reacted, they take that as a sign you have permitted and thereby encouraged the intimacy. If later you were to accuse them of sexual harassment, they would express amazement and say they were 'just being friendly'.

A pattern can be so ordinary, so universal, it is not identified.

We are living in the first time in history when human beings have a general picture of where we came from and a general picture of where we are going.

There is the cry for help, and there is the laugh for help.

People want to be explained to themselves. Which is why, to get a reaction, they occasionally cause strife.

The difference between art and the other professions is that anyone can call themselves an artist and be described as an artist by others. In an attempt to give objectivity and standards to artistic endeavour, art schools and academic qualifications have proliferated. Art schools can, ideally, be of help to the artist, but they are ultimately ludicrous because art, by its very nature, cannot be objectively standardised. Art is always a matter of aesthetics. Aesthetics is judgement of balance. Judgement is subjective.

The nicest thing we can say about many people is that they are misguided.

A man cannot be a Feminist. A man can be a Pro-Feminist.

What a sweet fancy: God having a mother.

You have to be a politician to better understand how politics works. It is immature to expect politicians to instantly act in accordance with your mercurial opinions and emotional states. In an ideal Democracy, each citizen is a politician.

Vulgarity is the being of Democracy.

Prayer is a form of self-deception, verging on self-hypnosis, which is employed by human beings to invoke magic, either in public ritual or when an individual knows there is nothing else that can be done. It has not been observed to occur in the other animals.

A writer cannot dictate what the words communicate, however hard the writer tries.

Imagination is the ability to manipulate memory.

We appear to be accustoming ourselves to Mars. First we used our imagination.

Visionary art protests at its surroundings.

We curate our bowel movements.

The eye likes to travel; the eyelid likes to shut.

The instinct to protect becomes the wish to possess.

Extinction is the norm.

If a person diagnosed with a life-threatening disease refuses treatment, would that be considered suicide?

It is not that a lot of men hate women; it is that they regard them the same way as they regard their dogs.

Christmas is Christianity's big opportunity to plead innocence.

Some galaxies are pulling away from ours, others are drawing closer; gravity is always a force in the Universe.

The wind can unpick padlocks, given enough time.

You are pursued throughout your life by a messenger who wants to give you a black envelope. With your last breath, you open the envelope.

How many billion galaxies are there? In 1919 we knew of only ours.

The futility, or, at least, the absurdity of existence, and the knowledge that the only alternative is non-existence; this is the fact which most humans are, understandably, unwilling to accept.

Gardening is choosing when to nurture and when to kill.

Only successful suicides are socially acceptable.

A cynic is someone who tells the truth too often.

On the stages of sexual love. First, the supreme pleasures of physical intimacy. Second, the struggle for power and control. When these two warring egotists reach a compromise, it's called 'relationship' or 'marriage'. Third, waning and loss of interest. Fourth, finished, due to non-practice, separation, divorce or death. Result: Children or no children.

Love is the blind love of a parent for its child. The other uses of the word 'love' are synonyms for 'peace'. All our lives, in all our encounters with others, we seek to be that child again.

Best to keep busy, even if only lighting candles and blowing them out.

The past is interesting, it's a hobby. The future is hard work.

Choosing between a comma and a semi-colon has to be faced with existential stoicism.

Talking to candles: "Do you see the beauty of this lit one? I want you all to aspire to that."

Socialists devote their energy to upgrading people from the under-classes to the over-classes. Population-growth is perpetual, so never more than a proportion of people get upgraded.

Due to population growth, there are more and more people in the under-classes and more and more people in the over-classes. In other words, more poor and more rich. It is plain that the rich offer a better chance for the survival of our species because they have the money, the education and the power.

The family is the enemy of free-thinking.

Both scientists and philosophers expect to be challenged because that is how ideas develop.

The history of the human race is the history of bullying.

It is not that God does not exist, but that God is meaningless.

Pro-Choice Religionists and Anti-Choice Atheists are equal cowards.

Atoms of truth can be contained in only one sentence at a time.

The individual always depends on others. How else can corpses be disposed of?

When someone suicides, the first question asked is how he or she did it. This suggests a practical interest in the matter.

Cliché is a fungus that thrives on originality.

Words like ‘truth’, ‘meaning’, ‘reality’ are transportation words. They are vessels that carry us onwards. They have no essence.

To break the rules of art, it is necessary to break the rules of society. Few would-be artists are capable of doing so.

Someone once famously said that death for the artist is a career move. Actually, it is more of a marketing strategy.

Art may come to be viewed as a primitive form of Artificial Intelligence.

All proffered philosophical systems are driven by personal psychologies.

It would be generous to say that the word 'sacred' is eulogistic, when tosh it is.

Everyone is at it: manipulating history.

We will eventually drop the word Artificial and simply call it Intelligence.

It is when one relaxes that one appreciates beauty.

Why do men try to control women? It is the nature of their sexuality.

What do men want? Apart from riches and everlasting fame, they want to be understood by women.

Religion is a form of mass-hypnosis. Not everyone can be hypnotised, as Freud quickly discovered. Both religion and hypnosis depend on the want-to-believe of the subject.

Love is when someone condemns you to live.

You cannot simultaneously sing and think.

Art is one answer to philosophy's question: what to do with time?

Philosophy is a study pursued by philosophers on behalf of others who do not have the intellect, will or time to philosophise. A philosopher is someone at work on the case, though there are no clues and the trail's cold.

There are liberals, there are conservatives, and there are the poor.

Political philosophies are constructed on ignorance of human nature.

Democracy is delicate. It cannot grow without rational education.

Philosophy, when it stands alone, unconnected with action, is little more than a bourgeois luxury.

For many centuries in Europe, women were described as the more promiscuous of the sexes. This, of course, was a tool of subjugation, intrinsic to religion, and a cop-out clause in men's guilt.

Logic is reason described by language. Mathematics is reason described by symbols.

Mediocre artists find themselves; great artists lose themselves.

An artist struggles to present truth-beauty; a gardener is presented with truth-beauty.

A writer is an engineer of sentences.

To slip by the guardians of untruth, you have to be ignored.

Mismanagement is the problem. It is not the workers' fault.

The word 'environment' puts humans at the centre. It is the natural world which is disappearing, not just our environment.

Writing is about language.

All experience is of equal relevance.

We cannot see reality, just as we cannot see the backs of our heads.

We are the result of cause and effect. Why bring purpose into it?

Many people will say that their religion-classes in childhood were a form of brainwashing, but it doesn't strike them that their history-classes were also.

Jazz is joy in loneliness.

In photography, the drawing is done for you.

The citizens have not been educated to Democracy. Too many people know more about The Bible, Koran et al, than they do about how their Government works and the State functions.

All priests abuse children.

An extrovert is an actor who has become the role.

With the advances in Physics, has Metaphysics been revealed as a phantom?

A writer is always quoted out of context.

A speaker is always quoted out of context.

Illiteracy is a cancer. It kills communication.

No matter what you do, you still end up in the present.

The monotony of the sea. Each wave's fall, withdrawal. Nothing to add or subtract from the sound of the sound. Nothing to name, nothing to save.

Slapdash dashlap shslap dash dash slap. Slapdash lap sh lap shslap. Slapdash sh dash lap. Sh dash lap sh dash.

A short story in four words: "I knew someone once." And another: "Woke up this morning."

Art is a family of languages.

There is no such thing as a bad photograph. A photograph is always a picture of light.

The Universe is not finite because a limit means there is something beyond the limit. And an infinite Universe is not mentally graspable.

We are the first known species to observe, study and calculate our own extinction.

Given the feebleness of present measures to curb population-growth, seeking a way to migrate from this planet is realistic and constructive.

At best, we can say that 'God' is what we do not know. If everyone would agree that 'God' is a word, there would be more peace on Earth.

One can never over-estimate the ignorance of another person.

We live out our lives by best-by dates.

To be a painter is to almost see; the painter is blind.

Truth is an edition of reality.

Everything happens on time. (That's 'on', not 'in'.)

What distinguishes the genuinely mad is that they have lost their sense of self-preservation.

Better a stable Dictatorship than a sham Democracy? No.

We cannot stop the destruction of the natural world, but we can slow it down.

Do not blow at the candle; open your mouth and, holding one hand behind the flame, eject a cough-like breath.

To ascribe purpose to the Universe is to belittle the Universe.

The living are celebrities among the dead.

You are awake, that is all it means.

Making art provides its own reward. It is not the pleasure principle, it is the surprise principle. Art's reward to its maker is surprise.

Surprise is the sister of innocence.

What has to happen will happen, but it can only have to have happened after it has happened.

If philosophers are scientists, are scientists philosophers?

The social code is always out of date.

If you think you do not have the right to help a suffering person to die, a person who wants to die, why do you think you have the right to keep alive a suffering person who does not want to live?

In mathematics, to explain and to predict are one.

Democracy versus Human Rights.

Human Rights versus Democracy.

There are three appearances of truth: scientific, philosophic and poetic. If one does not satisfy, it is because it does not exist independently of the other two.

All philosophers are saying the same thing: ideas exist.

Ideas exist amorally, until put into action.

At its core, what religion wants to do is subvert Democracy.

Art is born from liberation.

Throw a rock. Don't get caught.

Spring, that time of year when fools venture forth from their urban burrows to accelerate the destruction of the natural world.

Freud famously declared that he could not understand what women want. What a stupid man. Here's what women want: autonomy, control over their own selves. Is that too much to request?

Democracy needs be a school subject.

Too many people, not enough time to educate.

Quit while ahead? Jump while ahead.

Be brave, don't pray.

All is accident. The sense of it is subjective.

Indifference is intrinsic to survival.

Those who can write can change the names of things.

The best and the worst we can say are the same: "I am alive."

Originality is honesty.

An experience never happens twice. No wonder we wonder what it's all for.

The garden is the growing, dying garden growing.

It is the unpredictability of others that shocks.

"All the world's a stage, and all the men and women merely players…" Merely?

We don't like being put in harnesses, we want to be wild horses.

The price of a great friendship is its loss.

"How are you keeping?"

"I'm not keeping."

Be organised. Put that screwdriver back in its place.

No one is ahead of their time.

Once you get to fifty, it's all uphill.

Artists make art because they have nothing better to do.

Is it possible to see without the vanity of belief?

A person is not a genius, but something a person does can be distinguished by what we call genius.

The artist cannot be a slave to any political agenda, but that does not mean the artist is apolitical.

An abstract painting is asking the viewer to participate.

We are all scatterbrains.

There are the worlds in our heads and there is the world. None of us can access the world because we are in the worlds in our heads. Of course, there is interaction between the worlds in our heads and the world. That's called comedy.

THE VERSE

On a horse

with fixed eyes,

there you go,

there you go

on the merry-go-round,

with bared teeth.

"Yakkity yakkity yakkity yak."

Clappity clappity clappity clap.

The robin comes
to hide behind your hands
its one eye, its two eyes
behind the handle of your hoe.

The robin's gone,
there's a space
the robin hopped from.

The robin comes –
but no, you can't be
as still as a statue, so,
hoe on, on, on.

"Hence,"

he said aloud

and sat and wrote it down:

"Hence,"

his mind all over the place

hungry mirrors hold his face

that

plastic bag

not like anything else

but itself

in shreds

spread

in branches over

the roaring water

beyond

the constellations

the darknesses

where stars appear

to appear

disappear

plural of far

www.ingramcontent.com/pod-product-compliance
Ingram Content Group UK Ltd.
Pitfield, Milton Keynes, MK11 3LW, UK
UKHW020424310726
14060UKWH00021B/24